To my parents, Don and Nina Harrington, who made my recovery possible. Also to Mike and Kathy Roaleen whose friendship I cherish.

Acknowledgements

Thanks to Mike and Kathy Roaleen, Barb Koetsier, and Theoris Hall for reviewing the manuscript for this book. Their help is much appreciated.

Contents

Introduction

As you will learn by reading this book, clinical depression is an insidious disease. It affects not only the afflicted, but their friends and families.

The social costs of depression are astronomical. Treatment can be long and expensive and other costs include lost wages, divorces, disrupted relationships, and the misery of living with the disease.

This book focuses not on a single case of depression, but rather offers a guide to managing the disease and mapping a road to recovery. Case studies are used to illustrate key topics. Although the names have been changed to protect privacy, these are real cases.

In this book, the reader will find hope because depression can be overcome. It isn't an easy task, but it can be done. This hope is real—as the case studies illustrate. It is the desire of the author that people with depression and their family and friends will build on this hope and turn it into recovery.

This book is written by a survivor—one who suffered with major depression for six years. This book focuses on practical strategies that can lead to recovery.

Each person is unique and so are mental illnesses. Just as each case of depression is unique, so are the strategies to manage the disease. But there are commonalities. The strategies offered here should be viewed as suggestions—ones that can be altered to suit individual needs.

Finally, recognize that you have taken the first step to recovery by reading this book. Acknowledging the problem and then making the decision to feel better is important to recovery. This book is your guide to that path.

I hope to meet you on that road back!

Steve Harrington

What Is Wrong With Me?

I couldn't shake the loss of a close family friend and I had been crying for nearly a month. I slept most of the day and had lost interest in everything. When I wasn't sleeping I stared at the television and sobbed. Even my favorite programs failed to interest me.

My behavior was taking its toll on my teenage son. Jason was concerned and sometimes offered sympathy and sometimes told me to "just snap out of it." I was losing weight because I couldn't muster the energy to cook. Jason was living on Lucky Charms cereal. My consulting business was suffering and so was Jason.

I was feeling guilty about the unfairness so I mustered the energy to travel 60 miles to the nearest movie house to treat Jason to a matinee. On the highway, trouble started.

Make a plan. Don't let them get away with it. Make a plan.

I turned to Jason. "Did you hear anything? Don't let who get away with what?"

"I didn't hear anything. What are you talking about?"

A few miles down the road the voice returned, louder and more persistent this time. *Make a plan! Don't let them get away with it. Make a plan! Make a plan! Make a plan!*
I focused on the road ahead and turned up the radio. Above the silly heavy-metal rock music my son loved, I could still hear the voice.
Make a plan! Make a plan! Make a plan!
Suddenly, lines on the highway ran together and the roof of my SUV appeared to move. My son grabbed the wheel and steered us to a stop on the shoulder. "What's wrong?" he pleaded.
I was petrified. I knew, then, I was mentally ill and started to cry.
We never made it to the movie house. Instead, we went to a mental health agency and I began a long, torturous journey of recovery that endures a decade later.
I was hospitalized three times and rode a bumpy road to wellness. The voices and hallucinations stopped and eventually I was able to peer through the hopelessness and see opportunities.
In the course of my journey, I discovered I was not alone. Twenty million people suffer from clinical depression each year. I am one of those statistics.

Depression as a Disease

Clinical depression is a disease just as diabetes is a disease. Like diabetes, treatment for depression often takes many months or years.

Unlike diabetes, it takes mental "work" to overcome the disease.

Everyone has periods of depression. Most often these "blue" feelings last a few days and pass. But for some, depression lasts several weeks, months, or more and can cause people to lose energy and interest in things they once enjoyed.

Clinical depression is defined differently by experts but if you are depressed for more than two weeks, it *may* be time to consult a professional. You *may* be able to get help from your family physician or a local mental health agency.

If you answer yes to several of the following questions, it *may* be time to seek help:

Clinical Depression Self Test

- Do you have persistent feelings of sadness, emptiness, pessimism, or anxiety?

- Do you feel helpless, hopeless, guilty, or worthless?

- Is it difficult to make decisions, concentrate, or remember?

- Have you lost interest or pleasure in everyday activities? Have you dropped hobbies or activities?

- Have you lost your drive or energy? Do you seem to have "slowed down"?

- Do you have sleep problems (insomnia, early-morning waking, oversleeping)?

- Is your appetite increasing or decreasing?

- Do you have headaches, stomachaches, or backaches? Do you have chronic aches and pains in your joints and muscles?

- Are you restless or irritable?

- Do you want to be alone most of the time?

- Are you drinking or smoking heavily, or are you taking other drugs?

- Do you think about death, or about suicide?

- Do you have difficulty concentrating?

- Have you had difficulty functioning at work?

- Have you recently suffered a significant loss (death of a loved one, etc.)?

- Are you suffering from chronic pain or loss of function?

Clinical depression cannot always be recognized by the sufferer. Sometimes it takes the advice of family and friends to understand all is not well.

It is estimated that more than 60 percent of U.S. residents suffering from clinical depression are not treated appropriately. This is because symptoms are not properly recognized as clinical depression. Depression symptoms are sometimes blamed on a personal weakness, symptoms are so disabling that one cannot reach out for help, and symptoms are not properly diagnosed and treated.

Clinical depression can hit anyone. It does not respect any population segment although there is some evidence that people of color may be somewhat more susceptible to the illness.

It is important to recognize that stigma may play a large role in the failure to obtain assistance with any mental illness. One needs only to watch television to see the mentally ill portrayed as perpetrators of violent crimes.

This is unfortunate because studies show the mentally ill, when properly treated, are no more likely to commit crimes than the general public.

Clinical depression may appear as moodiness, anger, and isolation among adolescents. If you notice a change in an adolescent's behavior, consider depression as a possible cause.

What Causes Clinical Depression?

Researchers are still studying the causes of depression but there are clues that indicate a disruption of key electrical impulses in the brain.

For many years, researchers believed it was the lack or reduction of certain brain cell chemicals that caused depression. Specifically, they focused on low levels of seratonin and related chemicals. New medications have been developed to boost seratonin levels. Although it may take months, these medications seem to have a positive affect.

Recent research, however, indicates a more complex cause. Researchers have discovered that brain cell "receptors" may be damaged and depression can be cured only when these receptors heal.

Receptors accept electrical impulses from other brain cells and transfer them to yet other brain cells. While new brain cells cannot be created, these receptors can heal over time. Increased seratonin levels may help the brain heal receptors.

This new theory of the cause of depression is exciting because researchers can now develop new medications that focus on receptor healing in addition to boosting seratonin levels.

But what causes these changes in brain cells and their chemistry?

The answer is not clear although some research indicates that prolonged, deep depression can lead to clinical depression. Thus, it is not surprising for those who have lost loved ones to suffer clinical depression. Issues such as legal problems, divorce, loss of relationships, physical and sexual abuse (even as a child), grief, serious physical illness, and job loss can also lead to depression.

Clinical depression can also be caused by chronic pain, trauma (including childhood abuse), and the loss of function.

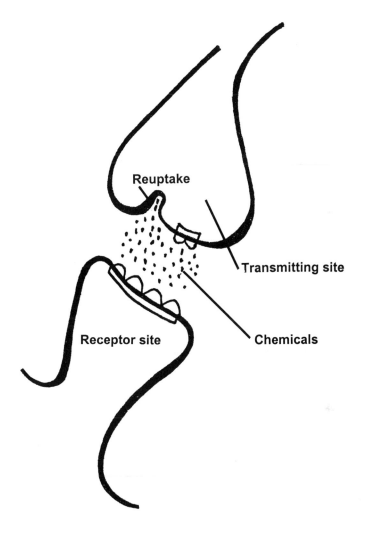

Reuptake

Transmitting site

Chemicals

Receptor site

It takes only 1/5000 of a second for an electrical charge to bridge the gap between neuro-transmitters. Note that they are bathed in important chemicals linked to clinical depression.

Consider the case of Frederick:

Frederick was severely wounded in the Gulf War. He lost the use of his left leg and arm when a land mine blew up.

Despite his physical challenges, Frederick earned a law degree. But the state bar declined to admit Frederick to the bar. They said he had unresolved anger issues that caused clinical depression. Without a license to practice law his dreams were shattered.

Frederick consented to psychotherapy and eventually worked through his anger. His depression subsided and he was granted a license to practice law.

Frederick's case also points out the role of anger in causing clinical depression. Some therapists say depression is "anger turned inward". This means that misplaced emotions can have a profound affect on the brain.

Counseling sessions often deal with how anger and other emotions (such as grief) are expressed. These sessions, if successful, can help a person live a happier and more productive life.

Clinical depression may also be linked to genetics. There is a growing body of evidence that points to a hereditary nature of the illness. This means that parents and grandparents who have suffered clinical depression may pass on the predisposition for the disease.

In some cases, clinical depression appears "idiopathic," that is, there is no apparent cause.

These cases are especially difficult because it is hard to understand the illness if no origin can be identified.

While many individuals suffer only a single bout of depression, some have chronic symptoms that can last for years. Still others recover wholly or in part only to suffer relapses. It is likely that those who suffer long periods have not received adequate counseling in dealing with the thought patterns that contribute to depression—an issue that will be covered later in this book.

Manic Depression (Bi-polar Disorder)

Manic depression, or bi-polar disorder, is a relatively common mental illness. It is characterized by periods of great elation or energy (mania) followed by deep depression.

Although bi-polar disorder is a separate illness from depression, the information contained in this book applies to those who are suffering the depression cycle of the disease.

It is important to note that both clinical depression and bi-polar respond well to medications and there is great hope for recovery from both illnesses.

Join the Crowd

Research shows that as many as 20 percent of U.S. residents will suffer clinical depression in their lifetimes. This is a huge number (1 in 5 persons).

There is some evidence that women suffer from clinical depression at a higher rate than men. This is because, researchers say, women tend to dwell more on problems whereas men are more likely to shrug them off.

Instead of acknowledging their feelings, asking for help, or seeking appropriate treatment, men may turn to alcohol or drugs when they are depressed, or become frustrated, discouraged, angry, irritable and, sometimes, violently abusive, according to the National Institute for Mental Health.

Some men deal with depression by throwing themselves compulsively into their work, attempting to hide their depression from themselves, family, and friends; other men may respond to depression by engaging in reckless behavior, taking risks, and putting themselves in harm's way.

Elderly men who were once the primary wage earner may suffer depression as a result of retirement. They have not fully come to accept their aging. Older males have the highest rate of suicide—not the young as many believe.

Persons who have suffered from depression include, singer Janet Jackson, football great Terry Bradshaw, and comedians Jonathan Winters and Robin Williams. Winston Churchill suffered from depression and called it a "black dog" that followed him through life.

Actress Patty Duke, Presidents Richard Nixon and Abraham Lincoln, and writer William

Styron are also among those who have suffered from depression.

It is important to note that even though these people suffer (or have suffered) clinical depression, they have succeeded in living productive lives. In many cases, depression can be overcome with a combination of medications and therapy. And, for many, the simple decision to change to a more mentally healthy lifestyle can have a profound affect.

Types of Depression

Just as it is with people, each case of clinical depression is unique for each person. As a result, recovery is also unique to the individual.

What follows are some general types of depression. You may find yourself in this information but it could be that you will not. This information is presented only as a way to categorize most types of clinical depression.

Major depression with psychotic features

In addition to feeling sad and hopeless, this type of depression is quite severe and is characterized by delusions and/or hallucinations.

The delusions may vary but often are related to financial matters. Delusions can also be persecuting, that is, they could make a person feel guilty of something they are not.

The hallucinations generally involve voices but can also include visual hallucinations such as moving walls and ceilings.

When a person recovers from this type of depression, the delusions and hallucinations generally subside.

Chronic major depression

This category of depression refers to those who have been continuously depressed for at least two years. This is a serious form of depression and is characterized by much frustration and guilt. It often takes many months of professional therapy, medication, and a strong commitment to get well for recovery.

Persons with chronic major depression frequently lose hope. For this reason, it is important that they meet others who have suffered with depression and recovered. They are prime candidates for support groups.

Major depression with melancholic features

This form of depression makes one feel nothing is worth doing. Persons suffering from this type of depression lose all interest in enjoyable events and activities, which is called anhedonia. This type of depression is commonly diagnosed among older persons.

Major depression with catatonic features

This type of depression is characterized by odd movements or a lack of movement of the body. Persons suffering from this type of depression may imitate voices and movements of others. Also, they may be too confused to respond well to questions.

Atypical depression

People suffering from this type of depression can be cheered up when good things happen to them. But then they quickly "crash" and may go into a catatonic state. This type of depression often causes people to eat great quantities of food and gain weight. Sufferers may also sleep a lot and take rejection badly.

This type of depression is often diagnosed among younger people.

Dysthymic disorder

People suffering from this type of depression often feel they have been depressed for a very long time, even though it may not have been that long. They struggle to function at work and in social situations. As many as 25 percent of the people suffering dysthymic disorder go on to experience major depression. This is sometimes referred to as "double depression."

Involutional depression

This is a type of major depression often found in elderly persons and can arise without any apparent cause. This type of depression can cause confusion, memory loss, and sleeping trouble.

Seasonal affective disorder

This disorder is often referred to as "S.A.D." People with this type of illness generally become depressed during the late fall and winter. In the summer, sufferers may find they have more energy.

Recent research indicates that S.A.D. is more common in northern climates where there is a greater differentiation in seasons. The amount of sunlight absorbed by the body seems to play a role with this type of depression.

Some sufferers report recovery through the use of full-spectrum light therapy. Another strategy is to get outdoors for at least a half-hour each day. Note that the sunlight reflected by snow increases the positive effects.

Depression (or mania) with postpartum onset

This type of depression is often diagnosed within four weeks of delivering a baby. There can be mixed episodes of depression and mania. There may also be delusions about the health of the baby.

New mothers with this type of depression may lose interest in their babies, have panic attacks, or cry for no apparent reason. Feelings of guilt are also very common.

Fortunately, this type of depression responds well to psychotherapy although medications are sometimes required. Note that the range of medications available to treat this type of depression may be limited if the mother is nursing.

Reactive depression

This type of depression is a reaction to a stressful or serious event, including legal trouble, grief, trauma, and other upsetting life events. It may be associated with other mental illnesses and is often considered a "normal" response to overwhelming hardships.

There is considerable hope for even the most depressed among us. Each year, many recover from this dreaded disease. But remember that once recovery is achieved, one must continue to work to avoid a relapse. Thus, the strategies in this book may require repetition.

Acknowledging the problem is the first step toward recovery. Some people live years with severe depression; unwilling to concede they could be happier. Still others come to live with depression as part of their lives not knowing life could be better.

Because you are reading this book, you most likely have taken this first step. Congratulations.

Why Do I Feel This Way?

Sarah was having a bout with major depression. She wanted to spend most of her time alone and was often irritable. When she was with people, she became angry for no apparent reason. Friends and family quickly became discouraged and stopped trying to help her.

Sarah was afraid to admit she had an illness. She believed time alone would solve her problems. But it didn't. She began sleeping most of the day away and lost her job as a store manager.

As more problems arose, Sarah became even more angry. Finally, Sarah swallowed her pride and saw a psychiatrist who diagnosed her as having clinical depression.

The psychiatrist prescribed anti-depressants and Sarah sought counseling that helped her deal with the turmoil in her life that contributed to her depression.

Why is it that we have these feelings?

Researchers still do not understand how the brain works but it is certain that when something goes awry with this organ, our whole lives can change radically and quickly.

A variety of feelings are commonly associated with clinical depression. Here are some feelings you may experience:

- **Anger**—Depression robs one of the ability to function normally. It is natural to be angry about the losses one suffers because of the illness. For many people, clinical depression has caused the loss of friends and family and in some cases material possessions—even jobs. All of these factors-- and because so much has been lost--are reasons to feel angry.

   How one deals with this anger can frequently have a profound affect on the course of the disease. Anger is a natural emotion and it is healthy to express that anger. But people who fail to learn how to "re-channel" their anger into positive energy will have a more difficult time recovering.

- **Fear**—Depression makes one feel out of control. This loss of control is often frightening. The first step in dealing with this fear is understanding that depression will not last forever and that fear is a normal reaction.

- **Frustration**—Some people respond to clinical depression with frustration. It is normal to want to be the person you once were. Depression seems to always affect the "best" part of you, leaving you wondering what part of your life will be affected next.

Contributing to this frustration is the length of time recovery often requires. We are accustomed to "quick fixes" and we must be mentally prepared for a long recovery period. For some, this recovery is months, for others, it can be years.

Frustration is especially difficult to deal with because there are no quick and easy answers to the disease. We can only work hard to prevent falling deeper into depression and strive to make the most out of life while we work to recover.

Avoid the temptation to self-medicate with alcohol or illegal substances. Many, many people with depression fall into this trap. As a result, they fall deeper and recovery is postponed.

- **Anxiety**—Anxiety seems to go hand-in-hand with serious depression. While there are medications available to treat this anxiety, the best results seem to come when depressed people learn to cope with anxiety.

  There are many ways to cope with anxiety and these will be discussed later in this book.

- **Fatigue**—Again, researchers still do not understand all of the workings of the brain so there is no clear answer as to why clinical depression so often brings on fatigue.

It is important to understand that feelings of fatigue are part of the depression. Very frequently, this fatigue makes it difficult to participate in normal activities and can have a serious detrimental affect at the workplace.

Some believe sleeping is part of the healing process. But at some point, the depressed person must take his/her own life in their hands and not be crippled by the disease. Excessive sleep can increase depression.

We will cover motivation issues later in this book but it is important to know at this point that fatigue is a very natural feeling. Also know that, with work, it can be managed.

- **Sadness**—Clinical depression can make one feel profoundly sad for no apparent reason. We may cry easily and for long periods without understanding our feelings of sadness.

  Eventually the sadness subsides as we regain control over our lives. Remember this is not a permanent feeling and will pass with time.

- **Hopelessness**—Hope is a powerful word. It is an incentive to go on—to keep on going to reach goals. But with clinical depression, the lack of hope is a common feeling and it can have devastating effects.

There is no magic that can bring hope into one's life, but hope can re-emerge if you are looking for it. In some cases, you find it where you least expect it.

- **Guilt**—This is probably the most destructive feeling associated with clinical depression. Family and friends—although well-meaning—often contribute to feelings of guilt by trying to encourage you to get better.

  Guilt is also a common feeling among those who are unable to muster the energy to be active. The feeling also arises when normally independent persons find themselves asking for help from family and friends.

  There is little we can do about these feelings of guilt except to try as well as we can to recover. Family and friends can be educated but, unless they've suffered the same illness, cannot fully understand the disease.

  Realize that guilt is a common feeling and can be discussed with those around you.

- **Isolation**—Clinical depression seems to rob one of family and friends just when they are needed most. Their lack of understanding of the disease can make things worse.

  The best approach is to educate family and friends as much as you can. Help them see that you are ill and will not always mean what you say. It is also important to give them some hope. Tell them you are sick but are fighting to get better and become the person you once were (or better!). Once they understand your efforts, they will be more patient.

Consider Emily's story of isolation:

Emily began suffering clinical depression for no apparent reason. She was an attractive, outgoing person but gradually began spending more and more time alone in her apartment.

Eventually, Emily lost a promising career, which only contributed to her depression. She felt hopeless and began gaining a considerable amount of weight.

At one point, Emily's mother could not tolerate the decline in her daughter's life and took action. Each morning Emily's mother went to Emily's apartment, got her dressed, and "forced" her to go out and face the day.

Emily's mother also made certain her daughter made and kept appointments for the psychiatrist and therapist.

At first, Emily was upset at her mother but soon began to enjoy the challenge of each new day. The mother and daughter planted a garden together and by the time the sweet corn was ripe, Emily was feeling better.

It took many months, but Emily eventually decided she could get better and made a commitment to work at it. Fear and isolation was replaced by determination and Emily was able to go back to work, thanks in no small part to her mother's positive influence.

These are only the most common feelings depressed persons feel. You may experience other feelings not listed here.

It is important to know that these feelings are natural with depression and, through recovery, can be overcome. Try not to be frightened or confused by these feelings. Instead, commit yourself to a course of action and develop a workable recovery plan.

How Do I Start To Get Better?

There is no "one way" to recovery. Just as each person is unique so is the depression they face. But there are commonalities that allow for general guidelines.

As mentioned before, acknowledging the problem is the first big step. It is surprising to learn that many people suffer from clinical depression and go undiagnosed due to fear.

Fear is a common emotion associated with depression. Depression is a mental illness and no one likes to admit they have such an illness. The stigma associated with mental illness can cost jobs, relationships, educational opportunities, even marriages.

The Decision

But we must get beyond stigma issues if we are to successfully treat depression. We must have the courage to admit we need professional help. Consider the case of Carl:

Carl was in his early 40s when his depression sent him to the hospital for the first time.

Carl was suicidal and in therapy disclosed that he had been depressed since he was a teenager.

After a few weeks of hospitalization, Carl gained ground and was discharged. Unfortunately, his depression quickly worsened after his discharge. Outpatient counseling helped Carl understand that he had a problem; to this he readily admitted.

Although Carl realized he had a problem and was willing to admit that it was greatly affecting his life, he was unwilling to take the next step—making the decision to get better.

"I don't like being depressed and I wish I could get better," he would say. But Carl fell short of making the decision. Perhaps he had been depressed so deeply and for so long that he was resigned to the notion that he would never recover.

Carl eventually became afraid to leave his home (agoraphobia) and, one day, was found dead of an apparent heart attack.

Carl's case illustrates how a person can become "trapped" by depression. It is an insidious disease.

This case also illustrates the fact that researchers are now learning that clinical depression can have profound, adverse effects on the body. For example, researchers have been able to make a link between depression and diabetes. There are growing bodies of evidence that point to depression as a potential cause of certain heart attacks and strokes. Doctors already know serious cases of clinical depression can shorten one's lifespan.

To make the decision to get better sounds deceivingly simple. The decision requires determination and personal insight. It is from this decision that all other advancement toward recovery flows.

Once you have made the decision, tell someone. This will reinforce your decision and make it more difficult to give up. Also, it is healthy for friends and family to hear you are interested in recovery. Telling them about your decision will be encouraging to them as well.

You may also want to set a deadline. Personally, I decided to give myself two years to start feeling better. Once I made that decision and set a goal, I found recovery came much faster.

Within six months after setting the goal I was feeling much better and became involved in volunteer activities. Volunteer activities led to a job offer and I soon discontinued anti-depressants altogether!

A potential problem with setting a deadline is failure. Set reasonable deadlines and don't "beat yourself up" if you fail.

About the time you make the decision to recover, you may want to consider keeping a journal. Writing daily activities, moods, thoughts, and feelings will help you recognize improvements. During especially difficult days, a journal can also serve as a reminder of better days and give you hope that life is not always as bleak as it may seem.

Blank journals, with a hard binding, are available at most office, stationery, and book retailers. But you don't have to get fancy to start and maintain a journal. Some people simply use 8 1/2 x 11-inch pads of paper.

Journals can take many forms. Perhaps the most useful for depression sufferers is an open letter to oneself. Try writing to yourself as though you were another person. These letters can be as personal as you wish because no one else will see them if you choose.

Writing itself is therapeutic. It provides an opportunity to express yourself in an open fashion and look at your disease in a more objective way. Although not always possible, try each day to identify events that make you feel depressed. Also try to identify events that have a positive affect.

A word of caution: you may not wish to share journal entries with friends and family because it may scare them unnecessarily. The darkness of clinical depression is well-known to the sufferer but may shock those unfamiliar with the disease.

Crisis Plan

Another consideration at this early stage of recovery is a crisis plan. Recovering from clinical depression can be a rocky road. Expect relapses. A crisis plan will help others assist you should you be hospitalized, go to a crisis home, or be incapacitated.

A crisis plan also ensures some control at a time when you may feel a loss of control. Having at least some control over your affairs can avoid anxiety and boost morale.

A crisis plan can include as much or as little information you wish. One of the key features of a good crisis plan is a contact list: who do you want to know about your illness? Be sure to consider spiritual advisors and key family members who will support you.

The following is an example of a crisis plan:

Crisis Plan

The following is my crisis plan should I require professional care. In addition to important information, this plan includes my wishes relating to my care.

If I require hospitalization, my preference is:

My psychiatrist is:_____

My social worker is:_____

My regular physician is:_____

In the past, I have been diagnosed with the following mental illness(es):

In addition to mental illness(es), I have the following health concerns:

My current medications and dosages are:

Medications that seem to work well for me include:

Medications that **do not** work well for me are:

I am allergic to the following medications:

I would like _____ to handle my financial affairs.

I would like _____ to care for my house in my absence.

I would like _____ to care for my children in my absence.

I would like _____ to care for my pets in my absence.

I (_____ would _____would not) appreciate visitors while I am hospitalized.

I would like the following people notified of my hospitalization:

_____	_____
Name	Phone
_____	_____
Name	Phone
_____	_____
Name	Phone

_____	_____
Signature	Date

Crisis plans should be given to family members, health-care providers, and/or close friends. Some people tape them to their refrigerators where they can be easily obtained by friends and family.

Consider whether to tell an employer you are hospitalized. Some employers can be very understanding while others are not. This is a judgment call for each individual.

Making the decision to recover is not as easy as it seems. This is especially true if addiction to drugs and alcohol are a problem fueling the depression. But after acknowledging the problem, making the decision to get better is the next big step. What follows is work. Hard work. But keep in mind that recovery is possible and it can happen for you.

The Crevice and the Dog

A bitter, cold rain bites my face.
It is dark. I cannot see.
And a silent danger lurks here.
I am in a steep crevice.
With each careful step I take,
I slip backward.

Even though I progress,
It seems as though I am falling deeper.
Into the terrible darkness.
I shout for help.
But no one is there.
I can stay where I am
But it frightens me.

Suddenly, below, I hear a dog.
It is growling and barking.
I can stay here,
But the dog.
The dog is getting closer.
I can stay here,
Or I can work.
Or I can work.

I try again with smaller steps.
I slip backward a little less.
It takes all my energy but I climb
And with each tiny step,

The dog falls away.
Then I see a glimmer.
Is it real or my imagination?

It hurts.
I cannot climb further.
But I do.
And the light is brighter.
I am near the top.
And I call out again.

This time, my friends and family
Call back. They are there—waiting.

They tell me to keep climbing.
And I do.
The light is bright.
And the dog…
I hear only wimpers.

--Steve Harrington

Where Do I Go From Here?

If recovery is to occur, so must work. This is not the everyday work where you clock in and out. This is a special type of work that undoubtedly seems easy for many but is difficult for the clinically depressed.

The work involves selecting small goals for each day and then building on those goals so one can move toward recovery.

No one said life is fair. No one said you wouldn't have to work hard in life just to share the happiness most others take for granted. But that is what clinical depression is all about.

The good news is that depression <u>can</u> be overcome. You <u>can</u> recover and enjoy life as you once did. Just as clinical depression strikes millions of people, so, too, do millions recover.

Clinical depression is a challenge and as novelist William Styron observed, much can be learned by overcoming that challenge. You will learn that you have the capability to overcome-not just depression-but other difficult challenges in your life. So, let's get started.

Select Small Goals

The first step in selecting goals is to understand that accomplishing even small tasks that would be considered routine when you are well, can seem insurmountable when you are suffering from depression.

Do not let the size of the goals bother you. Well-meaning friends and family may want to see you pick large goals because they want you to recover more quickly. But keep in mind that recovery from major clinical depression takes time. Start small and work up.

This is not an "easy" fix to a complicated problem. It is only the beginning. But once you have succeeded in selecting and attaining small goals, you can build on those goals and move toward recovery.

It is important to select small goals because failing to achieve large goals right away will only frustrate and could lead to deeper depression. Here are some examples of small goals that can be achieved on a daily basis:

- Take a shower
- Spend time outdoors
- Call or visit a friend or family member
- Write a letter
- Write in a journal
- Read a few pages of a book or magazine
- Take a walk
- Clean a small area of the house

- Go to the store
- Work in a garden
- Prepare a special meal
- Get dressed up
- Mow the lawn
- Shovel snow
- Go shopping
- Groom yourself
- Meditate
- Exercise
- Cook for someone else

Don't try to do it all at once. Pick only one small goal, if necessary, per day and strive to complete that goal.

After you have mastered a small goal for a week, pick another small goal and add that to the first. After a week or two of two small goals, pick a third and so on.

Soon, you will find that you are ready for more and more goals and larger ones at that.

Keep in mind that selecting and completing small goals is often the most difficult part of recovery. Pat yourself on the back each day you succeed. If you fail to succeed, don't lose hope. There is always tomorrow.

Make a Plan

Once you have mastered a few small goals it may be time to look at where you want to go with your life. And just as you want to start with small goals, so do you want to make a reasonable plan for your life.

Spend some time (perhaps as much as a week or more) to think hard about where you want to be in one year, two years, and five years from now. Again, do not pick difficult goals that are going to frustrate you. Start simple and build your confidence.

Select only three or four goals for each period and then think about what steps (objectives) must be taken to achieve those goals. Be sure to write them down and post them on a bedroom wall, refrigerator, or someplace else you can see them daily. Here is an example:

Year One

Goal: Find a job
        Objective: Write resume
        Objective: Search want ads
        Objective: Practice interviewing
        Objective: Apply for jobs

Goal: Buy a car.
        Objective: Save money
        Objective: Obtain driver's license
        Objective: Find car in price range

Goal: Maintain psychiatric stability
        Objective: See physician/psychiatrist
        Objective: Take medications
        Objective: Counseling
        Objective: Socialize

Year Two

Goal: Move into a new apartment
        Objective: Save money for security
                             deposit
        Objective: Find roommate
        Objective: Search housing ads
        Objective: Sign lease
        Objective: Pack belongings
        Objective: Find moving help

Goal: Maintain psychiatric stability
        Objective: See physician/psychiatrist
        Objective: Take medications
        Objective: Counseling

Year Five

Goal: Make new friends
        Objective: Socialize
        Objective: Join clubs/volunteer

As you can see, some goals may be repeated. Also, it is important to keep all goals in mind because it may take years to accomplish certain goals. For example, making new friends may be a five-year goal but one can start working on it before then.

Also be aware that goals often change. Be open to new ideas and the fact that new, more meaningful goals may arise.

How Do I Feel Better?

Goal setting is only one part of the recovery journey. Many sufferers need to know how to feel better while they are working on goals.

Again, there are no easy answers as each person is unique, but, perhaps, a combination of strategies could help. What follows are some ideas that have helped others feel better.

Educate Yourself

Educate yourself about clinical depression so you know what you are facing and can make better decisions about your treatment.

Read self-help books or listen to inspiring audiotapes. Look for treatment options and try to discover which ones may be best for you.

Find out what has helped others and keep in mind that many others have recovered. There is hope and looking for that hope will help you find it sooner rather than later.

Be Kind to Yourself

Celebrate yourself! Remember you are dealing with a disease not of your making (despite what well-meaning friends and family may say). Feelings of guilt are common among those who are depressed. Don't let those feelings frustrate or defeat you. Plan an event at least once each week just for you. Here are some ideas:

- Go to a movie
- Make popcorn
- Go to a tanning salon
- Get your hair done or get a haircut
- Visit special friends
- Go shopping
- Play bingo
- Fix a special meal
- Go out to eat
- Take a relaxing drive in the country
- Take up a new hobby
- Read a book
- Go to church
- Take a long, hot bath

Whatever you do, be certain it is something that will make you feel better. Don't wait until you feel like doing something to do it. Motivate yourself or perhaps nothing will happen at all.

Most of all, don't feel guilty about treating yourself to something special. Don't be afraid to have fun!

Pets

A puppy's wagging tail or a kitten's purr are sure to bring a smile. Consider adopting a cat or dog.

If your living situation makes it difficult or impossible to have a pet, consider making friends with a neighbor's cat or dog. Ask if you can "pet-sit" for a few hours a day.

Pets will also give you someone to talk to and they can bring their own challenges. Don't underestimate the value of having your mind pleasantly occupied by a pet. Every minute your mind is distracted from your illness the better it is.

Consider the story of Betsy who found living difficult after the loss of her husband:

Betsy discovered her husband's body hanging lifeless in the garage one morning. She was consumed by grief. Still, she managed to go to work each day but found it difficult to make friends.

Once a very social person, Betsy found herself alone each evening and on weekends. She purposely isolated herself because she believed no one would understand the profound sadness she felt.

One day, Betsy found a kitten at her doorstep. Reluctantly, she took the kitten in and gave it some milk. Betsy was taken by the kitten's loud purr and she decided to make a home for it. But Betsy worried about the solitary kitten at home all day long and feared it would get bored.

To solve this problem, Betsy went to the Humane Society and came home with another kitten for the first one to play with.

Suddenly, Betsy found her evenings and weekends filled by watching the two kittens play. Betsy found she had something positive to talk about at work. Her co-workers brought in small toys for the cats to play with and Betsy discovered new friends at her job.

Although Betsy was still saddened by the loss of her husband, she found new joy in the kittens' play. Betsy started socializing with co-workers and found she did not have to sit alone every night. Her life was much richer and eventually she started her own successful business. Her illness had actually strengthened Betsy and allowed her to take on new challenges with new-found emotional power.

Spirituality

For many, a belief in a higher power is important to their recovery. Not only do some sufferers find comfort in reading the Bible, but also in attending religious services. In addition, some find church organizations offer volunteer opportunities where they can find friends who share a common belief.

Most churches have staff trained in counseling; especially grief counseling. Some churches even reach out to the mentally ill by sponsoring special events and services.

What can religion offer? Prayer.

Pets can play an important role in recovery.

Many find prayer to be a welcome distraction to the profound sadness and negative feelings clinical depression often brings. Sufferers can pray for the pain to alleviate, strength to go on, and wisdom in selecting vital choices, such as good counselors and doctors.

Expressing one's feelings through prayer is also therapeutic. It takes careful thought to pray for healing and that thought can lead to the development of goals.

There are relatively few clergy who do not understand the problems of mental illness. In one case, however, a mentally ill person went to his pastor to explain the difficulties life had presented to him. Even though the person was a lifelong member of the church, the pastor told him to leave as he was possessed.

What can you do? Find a new church if clergy are not understanding. Mental health professionals are often aware of churches understanding of the problems faced by the mentally ill. Find one and explore how religion may help the healing process.

Keep in mind that Christianity is not the only religion. Try attending services of various religions to find one that suits you best. Consider inviting a friend to go with you in your exploration of spirituality.

Exercise

Exercise can be a powerful antidote to depression. Getting the body moving is not only healthy for the heart, but recent research indicates that favorable brain chemicals are created at a faster rate due to exercise. And a healthy, fit body is more fun and energetic.

Also, some medications are more effective when a person is active. Be aware that some medications can cause weight gain or weight may be gained as a depression symptom. Exercise will help you keep excess weight off.

Your exercise does not have to be an elaborate affair. A brisk walk can be healthy. But before you engage in strenuous exercise, you should be certain to contact your medical doctor for advice.

Diet

For nearly a century we have known that what we eat and drink affects our bodies. These foods can also have a profound effect on our brains. This means we must be careful about the quantity and quality of what we consume.

A good example is caffeinated coffee. While a single cup in the morning may not greatly affect our bodies, generally, multiple cups later in the day can easily disrupt sleep cycles.

Another example is alcohol. Even a single beer can affect brain function and this effect may be amplified when we take psychotropic medications such as anti-depressants.

Nicotine from cigarettes can affect how we feel. Although nicotine from cigarettes is a mild anti-depressant, there are many health hazards associated with smoking. Consider quitting.

The lesson here is one of extreme caution. It is best to abstain from alcohol, caffeine, and tobacco products. Eating healthy foods, such as fresh fruits and vegetables, not only makes us feel better, but can help us control our weight—a problem that can arise with certain medications.

Weight control for sufferers of clinical depression can be a problem not only because of the medication side-effects, but also because the disease robs one of self-discipline. It is not uncommon to see significant weight gains among sufferers who have little or no structure to their day.

On the plus side, taking a multi-vitamin daily can ensure that we are getting enough vitamins and minerals in our systems. Recent research indicates that increased doses of vitamin B_{12} can help the body fight depression.

The best approach is a healthy diet, limiting quantities of food, and exercise. Beware of "miracle" diet pills and supplements because these diet aids may contain chemicals that could have adverse effects when combined with common depression medications.

If you need help, consider Weight Watchers[TM] or similar clubs that have a proven track record and promote healthy eating habits. In addition to weight control, attending weight-loss classes will help you add structure to your day and provide you with an opportunity to meet new people.

Socialize

It is important to be around other people because socialization helps those with clinical depression keep their minds off their problems. It can also lead to new friends who can provide support during dark times.

Let's face it, no one wants to be around a depressed person who is constantly looking at the negatives of life. Instead, people like to associate with others who are positive and cheerful (note that it is possible to be cheerful to the point of annoying).

It may be the most difficult thing for you to do, but consider your attitude and adjust it in a positive manner so you are attracting people instead of driving them away.

It isn't necessary that everyone know your depression problem (in fact, some people may be "turned off" by your illness), but having at least one trusted friend with whom you can share your feelings can be important.

You may be able to find a listing of clubs through a social service agency or in the phone book. Another place to find out information about various clubs is through your local newspaper. Many newspapers feature stories and calendars of various clubs. If not, don't hesitate to call the editor to find out what is available.

Many clubs are focused on hobbies. If you don't have a hobby, consider starting one. If you need inspiration or more information about a hobby, simply go to a hobby shop and look around and ask.

Many hobby shops post club meetings and you might be surprised at how much you can learn and enjoy yourself.

Support Groups

In many communities, social service agencies—and even churches—offer free support groups geared specifically for those suffering from clinical depression.

Participating in a support group will help you realize that you are not alone. You may find that you have much in common with other people. Understanding that you are not the only one suffering from depression--and the often frightening feelings it brings—can be of great comfort.

Support groups frequently meet weekly but some meet more often than that.

The best support groups are ones that focus on feeling better and less on the problems of depression. Meetings that dwell on the negative aspects of clinical depression can lead to deeper depression so be careful.

It is a difficult balance because many seek help from support groups for specific problems. And, very often, the group can offer meaningful suggestions.

If you don't feel a group is helpful, find another one.

What if there is no support group where I live? Consider starting one. You don't need professional training to organize and lead a support group (although professional training doesn't hurt).

Churches and community buildings are often available at no charge. Remember to focus on solutions to problems and less on the problems themselves.

Stress Management

It is important to avoid stressful situations. Work, especially, can lead to stress. Remember that you have an illness and it is more important to recover than to get that next promotion.

Consider Frank's solution to stress at the workplace:

Frank worked for a social service agency and had a bout with major depression. Although he felt he had recovered and he liked his job, he felt considerable stress in dealing with clients all day long.

Frank tried different ways to relieve the stress but nothing seemed to work. The stress was so extreme that Frank felt he would have a relapse if he didn't get it under control. Finally, out of desperation, he started going to his car during lunch and coffee breaks.

In his car, Frank listened to soothing music on the radio and read books about pirates, religion, and nature; anything not related to his job. Soon, Frank discovered the stress disappeared. He was happier at work and managed to control depression symptoms.

While it is important to avoid stressful situations, it is also important not to let stress management become a means of isolation and brooding. Be certain you are managing stress for recovery and not contributing to a downward spiral of the disease.

Stress can be related to anxiety, which will be covered later in this book.

Volunteer

If you are unable to work, you may want to consider volunteering. Like a job, it will add valuable structure for the day and give you a reason to get out of bed and get going. Volunteering not only helps other people, but gives you the opportunity to meet new friends. Besides, helping others makes people feel good about themselves.

Here are some suggestions for finding volunteer opportunities:

- Schools
- Museums
- Hospice programs
- Libraries
- Goodwill
- Soup kitchens
- Botanical gardens
- Parks
- VFW facilities
- Hospitals
- Zoos

- Salvation Army
- Nursing homes
- Humane Society
- Food pantries

Note that some organizations have training periods with formal classes. These are opportunities to learn new things.

Other volunteer opportunities can involve no formal organizations—such as picking up litter along a roadside or park. Keep your mind open to new learning experiences!

How Do I Manage Symptoms?

Clinical depression brings with it a host of symptoms. While the number and severity of symptoms is likely to vary among individuals, there are some general guidelines for managing them.

Managing symptoms is important because if we let the symptoms control us, our depression will deepen. Consider Sharon's experience:

Sharon was a mother of two in her forties. Her husband suddenly left her and their young children alone. Adding to this pressure was the fact that Sharon received no child support because her ex-husband kept on the move and rarely worked a steady job.

Sharon was responsible and had a good job but the combined pressures of employment and family were dragging her down. Just as it looked like things couldn't get any worse, Sharon's mother died. The loss sent her into a tail spin.

Sharon fought depression on her own for several weeks but she finally decided that she needed help. Her physician referred her to a psychiatrist who prescribed anti-depressants. But Sharon was filled with anxiety.

She paced the floor, couldn't concentrate, and cried almost constantly when she wasn't working. Her psychiatrist felt additional medications for Sharon's anxiety would be inappropriate. Instead, he sent her to a therapist to learn relaxation techniques.

Although it was difficult for Sharon at first, she learned to spend time alone—away from the children and work—and listened to soothing music in a reclining chair.

Sharon also learned to recognize stressful situations that would exacerbate her anxiety. She avoided these situations and when she felt anxiety building, concentrated on "mindfulness techniques," which helped distract her.

Sharon's depression began to lessen and so did her anxiety. She was able to make it through some difficult years and eventually recovered completely. Today, Sharon still practices relaxation and mindfulness techniques to help her focus on difficult tasks.

Anxiety

Relaxation and mindfulness techniques can be valuable aids in reducing anxiety—a common depression symptom.

Relaxation techniques are strategies for reducing stress and focusing on relaxing the mind and body. For some, it may be simply closing eyes and listening to soothing music.

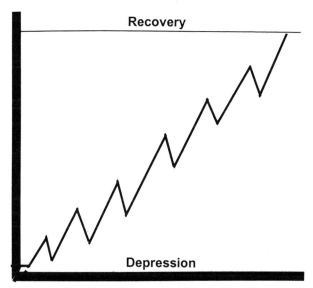

**The road to recovery is often bumpy.
Expect ups and downs along the way.**

Another relaxation method is borrowed from a type of hypnosis. The person listens to commands (which can be taped) to relax from toe to head.

Using a count-down from ten to one, the person is instructed to relax certain parts of the body. The countdown is repeated six or more times and the person eventually is totally relaxed. Many times, people fall asleep using this technique.

A post-sleep suggestion can be made that makes the person continue the relaxed state even after awakening.

Mindfulness is the art of using the mind to focus on something to the point where problems and stress are forgotten for the moment. A person's mind can be focused on something as simple as breathing.

To perform this exercise, find a darkened room, sit comfortably, and close the eyes. Concentrate on how your body reacts to breathing. Notice if one nostril is clearer than another. Concentrate on the sounds your body makes when breathing. Do this for five minutes or more. During this time you will find your mind is less stressed and anxiety fades.

Another mindfulness exercise is equally simple. Put a pencil or pen on a table and try to move the item with your mind. Visualize the item moving.

Mindfulness takes practice but once accomplished, it is much easier the second time. Soon, you can find yourself practicing during business meetings, riding the bus, or during similar activities.

If you are anxious about a particular problem, remember that problems can often wait and you are unlikely to solve the problem when you are in a negative mental state. In your mind, put the problem off until you are well rested.

When a decision about a problem is required, set a time limit to make the decision. Allot five minutes to make the decision and then spend the rest of the time planning ways to solve the problem.

Perhaps the most important aspect of problem solving is recognizing that not all problems <u>can</u> be solved. Understand that some things in life simply cannot be resolved by a single person.

Other suggestions for managing anxiety include keeping busy and finding someone to talk to. The goal is to distract oneself so the negative feelings do not have an opportunity to dominate thinking.

Excessive Sleeping

We will cover ways to "get up and get going" but some points are worth repeating.

Establish a regular schedule and make a plan for the day. Exercise during the day and ask for help when necessary. Mental health professionals may have other answers to this onerous depression problem.

Isolation

Look for opportunities to be with people. And work at real interaction. Note that you can be with people but still feel isolated if you are not interacting with them.

One of the best ways to start conversations is by complimenting people on what they wear or what they do. Ask follow up questions such as: "Where did you get that pretty sweater?"

Other suggestions for overcoming isolation are: take classes, be with family/friends, adopt a pet, volunteer, and job hunt. Consider joining a hobby club or serving an a church committee. These are all opportunities to meet people and make new friends.

Guilt Trips

It is not uncommon for those suffering from clinical depression to spend a considerable amount of time feeling a deep sense of guilt. As mentioned earlier, comments from well-meaning but ignorant friends and family can contribute greatly to this guilt.

Instead of dwelling on the guilt learn to shrug it off. Use positive self-talk to deal with these negative feelings.

Positive self-talk involves a mental exercise where one focuses on strengths. Some people even write a list of their strengths and refer to it during "down" times.

Another strategy is to talk to understanding people and if no one near you is understanding about depression, then make an effort to educate them.

Forgive yourself if you have made a mistake. It does no good to dwell on guilt. If you made a mistake, own it. Call the person(s) affected and apologize if you must.

Appetite

Depression often causes people to lose or gain weight. This can be prevented by planning meals carefully, exercising, eating more fruits and vegetables, staying away from junk food and caffeine, and not using food as a source of comfort.

Anger

Anger is often similar to guilt. When we don't want to feel guilty about something we often get angry instead.

Forgive yourself for feeling angry; there's nothing to feel guilty about. It is a natural emotion. Learn to handle your anger in a positive manner, such as punching pillows.

Don't hold long grudges. Grudges consume emotional energy you need for recovery.

Apologize if you have done or said something that offended someone. Own your mistakes—everyone makes them.

Probably the best strategy is finding someone to talk to. Verbalizing your feelings helps you understand them. This is especially true of anger. Try to be specific about why you are angry and explore what can be done about the situation.

Suicidal Thoughts

Suicidal thoughts are extremely common among the depressed. As many as 30 percent of depression sufferers will attempt or successfully commit suicide.

This is a sensitive subject but one we must cover because it is so important. Consider my own experience with suicide:

I had suffered enough. I had been in a deep depression for years. I carefully crafted a note detailing who would raise my son. I was going to do it. I simply had no hope.

I surveyed a cupboard and plucked a pill bottle that was half-full of a potent pain killer. I had thought about suicide before but this time I felt I had no choice.

I fingered the pills in my hand and thought about suicide again. Yes, I thought to myself, this is the only way out for me. The pills went down in three gulps and I laid down on my bed waiting for them to do their final work. I quickly fell asleep.

Two days later I awoke. I was disappointed. I didn't have enough pills to do the work.

For days I successfully kept my suicide attempt a secret. I destroyed the note and went on suffering as though nothing had changed. But something had changed.

I still felt hopeless but I surprised myself that I was so desperate. I thought about that desperation. It scared me. Scared me enough to think about what I had almost done and the disease that nearly overcame me.

Eventually, I mustered the courage to tell my parents. They were scared, too, and tried to get me to go back to the hospital.

But my desire to end it all passed. Logically, it was not the answer I sought. Instead, I decided not to let depression succeed in claiming another life. I gave myself two years to feel better.

I started volunteering, met new people, and finally decided I had something to offer this world. Somewhere, somehow, I found hope again.

When I think about those desperate times it seems like a dream. I shrug my shoulders at my almost-fatal confusion. These days, instead of hopelessness, I see opportunities.

Sure, my life isn't perfect but I am feeling like my old self again. No. I am feeling better than my old self. I am grateful I didn't have enough pills.

Today, when I counsel depressed people who think about suicide, I tell them my story. I tell them that no matter how dark life appears at the moment, they <u>can</u> and <u>will</u> get better if they leave their minds open and accept the challenges depression has brought them. I tell them suicide is permanent but depression is temporary.

There are many ways to commit suicide. That isn't the difficult part. What is difficult is facing life and all the problems it can bring. Make the decision that suicide is <u>not</u> an option.

But help is out there. Most communities have a suicide hotline and professional mental health workers are often available—even at night when life seems most challenging.

When suicidal thoughts arise, this is the time when it is most helpful to have people to talk to. That is one reason why socialization is stressed in this book. Talking about suicide and other problems associated with depression helps the sufferer process their feelings and look at them more objectively.

Holiday "Blues"

Be aware that depression symptoms often worsen during holiday periods. It is a time when people are celebrating and having fun. It is often difficult to be part of the merriment when you feel hopeless, frustrated, angry, and sad.

This is a challenging time and many depressed people get through the holidays by "putting on a face" and acting happy. That is not all bad because it forces one to think positive.

The best advice is to try to be positive and enjoy the holidays as best you can. Also, avoid negative situations during this time.

How Can Friends and Family Help?

The importance of understanding friends and family cannot be overstated. These people can provide the type of support that can be crucial to recovery.

The biggest obstacle facing friends and family is understanding. They often see the depressed person as lazy or simply moody. They fail to recognize clinical depression as a disease.

What friends and family need is education. Unfortunately, there is little material designed to educate them. Until now. If you are suffering from clinical depression, simply show them this book and encourage them to read it carefully.

But what can friends and family do to support you? Here are some ideas:

Attend Support Groups

Although many support groups are aimed at depression sufferers themselves, some groups are open to friends and family. Also, some support groups are geared specifically for friends and family and not those afflicted.

Be Optimistic

Depression is a disease that robs people of hope and fills them with negativity. People with depression may need someone to be optimistic for them. Remember that a great many people suffering from clinical depression achieve recovery every year and once again become happy, productive people. Proper medication, therapy, and a person's commitment to feel better are key to recovery so there is reason to be optimistic about the future.

Be Prepared for a Long Haul

Recovery is unique for each person. For some, this may take many months or even years. With support from friends and family, the time it takes for recovery can be decreased dramatically. So, hang in there!

Get Help Early

If you suspect you may be suffering from depression, let friends and family help you get the help you need. People with depression should see a family physician or psychiatrist as soon as possible. Learn to recognize symptoms early. Remember, the sooner a person is treated, the sooner they may recover.

Friends and family can provide much support for those suffering from clinical depression.
(photo by Jane B.)

Help with Medications and Appointments

Clinical depression often robs sufferers of short-term memory and creates confusion. People with depression may need help remembering to take their medications as prescribed. Also, they may need assistance in making and keeping appointments.

People with depression may realize they need help but are too frustrated, angry, or afraid to ask; most do not want to be a burden. The best approach for some may be to be "asked" if they need help. Loved ones can simply ask permission to be of assistance.

Help with Financial Matters

Again, clinical depression can cause short-term memory problems and confusion. People with depression may need help to organize financial matters. Loved ones can help by organizing bills, as they come due and help write checks or withdraw money from bank accounts. Because sufferers may have lost a job, it may take some negotiation with creditors; friends and family can help by dealing with creditors for late or reduced payments.

Include in Daily Activities

Even though they may sleep a great deal and complain of tiredness, persons with clinical depression still want to be as normal as possible. Friends and family can help by including them in daily activities. Shopping, running errands, or visiting friends can have a positive affect.

Friends and family should try to be as positive as possible and listen to problems. Loved ones don't have to have all the answers—just listen because telling how you feel will help others understand the disease.

Keep in Contact

Clinical depression tends to drive friends and family away just when they need them most. Remember people with depression may say things they don't mean so friends and family must be "tough skinned" if criticized. Friends and family should also be aware that you may be jealous of their wellness.

Friends and family should plan regular contact times during the week so it gives everyone something to look forward to. Include people with depression in special outings and don't let them drive away supportive people in their lives. Some day it could be them who needs help battling depression.

Understand the Illness

Friends and family should make an effort to truly understand that clinical depression is an illness. They should read the early chapters of this book to understand the physical causes of depression. They can also look for literature at doctor's offices and pharmacies about depression. Again, it helps to have someone listen to the person suffering from depression so that everyone understands how the disease is affecting the individual and them.

It is also important to understand that depressed people do not want to be a burden for others but they do need support; whether they ask for it or not. Friends and family shold be patient and

make a commitment to help the afflicted person
even if it takes a long time for recovery.

Don't Get Dragged Down

Don't let the depression of a friend or family
member drag down the people they need for
support. They will not be very helpful if they, too,
become depressed.

Yes, depression is a serious illness but
remember friends and family must be strong if they
are to be of help. Let them take a break from the
person with depression.

It is difficult to live with anyone who has a
chronic, serious illness and the same is true for
those suffering from depression. Remember they
may become irritable and say things they do not
mean. Friends and family must be tough-skinned
and patient but don't verbally attack them either.
Friends and family should set boundaries and stick
to them.

Again, it is a good idea for friends and
family to plan time away from the depressed so they
can return strong.

Beware of Stigma

Mental illness carries with it a societal
stigma. Think about all the negative ways we refer
to the mentally ill: crazy, demented, daffy, daft,
psychotic, looney, and crackpot to name a few.
People with depression are often called "lazy" by
those who do not understand the illness.

This stigma is pervasive and may cause the afflicted person to deny the illness. A better approach is to acknowledge the illness and deal with it.

Friends and family should try not to make negative comments about the person's mental illness and keep positive. Be aware that the depressed person may wish to keep the illness secret from the rest of the world.

Pray

Many persons—including those afflicted—find it useful to pray for recovery. Friends and family should not try to force their religious beliefs on the person suffering from depression but, instead, be supportive and offer spiritual assistance.

Many clergy are open to special counseling sessions and some churches have organizations to specifically deal with depression. Friends and family may suggest spiritual involvement but the sufferer should make his/her own decisions about this often personal issue.

Special Meal

Prepare a special meal or go to a restaurant once a week. This will provide a positive activity for the depressed person and help them keep their mind off their disease.

Attend Doctors' Appointments

Because of short-term memory problems, the depressed person may not comprehend or remember all that a physician or psychiatrist may tell them. For some people with depression, just getting out of the house can be overwhelming and encouragement will ensure that appointments are kept.

But keep in mind that friends and family should attend these appointments only with the permission of the person afflicted.

Attending these appointments will not only help friends and family help with medications, but it will also give them an opportunity to ask questions and learn more about the disease.

Understand Symptoms may not Always be Present

Many depressed people can gather their emotional strength and appear normal when they are around family and friends. Or, in some cases, depression symptoms are simply not present all the time. Help friends and family understand that how a person feels can change rapidly once they are alone.

Exercise

Exercising is difficult enough for healthy people and it can be excruciating for the depressed.

It can help a great deal to have someone around to exercise with. Exercising with a workout tape is always more fun with someone else or get creative and make up your own exercises.

Respect

Everyone likes to be treated with respect and it is no different for those suffering depression. People suffering from depression should be treated as equals, capable of making life decisions no matter how symptomatic they may be. Unless permitted by the person suffering from depression, friends and family should avoid the temptation to make decisions. People suffering from depression should be asked for input whenever possible.

Watch Other Family Members

Researchers believe there may be a genetic link with clinical depression. This is important because whole families can suffer the disease.

If one family member is afflicted, others may be genetically predisposed for the illness. Educate your family about depression and encourage them to talk about how they feel. Watch for symptoms early on, especially after the loss of a loved one through divorce or death, and get help as soon as possible.

Communicate

Communication is an important element in recovery. Expressing one's feelings about how depression is affecting their lives helps the sufferer process information and can "take a load off". Friends and family can help by encouraging that communication.

Find a place that is quiet and free from interruptions. That may be a local library or during a walk.

Avoid the blame game. Remember that depression sometimes occurs for no apparent reason so don't blame anyone for the disease and the destruction it has brought.

Don't argue. Promise yourself to "step back" if a discussion turns toward argument. Take a break and come back to the discussion later.

Avoid old issues and other problems. Focus on the depression and eventual recovery and less on problems. Encourage the family member or friend to try some of the recommendations in this book.

Attitude

Attitudes toward clinical depression and the loved one affected can go a long way in helping one achieve recovery. The National Alliance for the Mentally Ill (NAMI) has the following suggestions for friends and family:

- If your loved one is undergoing medication therapy, be sure the doctor's orders are followed. Encourage him or her to stick to the doctor's recommendations—any medication should be taken exactly as the doctor says.
- Keep the person separate from the illness. Love the person even if you hate the illness.
- It's not okay for you to neglect yourself— it's important for family members and friends to take care of themselves during this stressful time.
- The illness of a family member or friend is nothing to be ashamed of. Remind him or her (and yourself) that deciding to do something about depression is very courageous.
- No one is to blame.
- It's as hard for the individual to accept the illness as it is for his or her family members and friends.
- You alone cannot resolve depression for a family member or friend—it has to be your loved one's decision to work toward recovery.
- It's natural and acceptable to feel a mix of emotions such as guilt, fear, anger, and sadness when a loved one suffers from an illness.
- Learn all you can about mental illnesses.

- You and your family are not alone. Sharing your thoughts and feelings with friends or a support group can be very helpful.
- Be patient; remember that recovery doesn't happen overnight. It's a journey that's full of ups and downs. Encourage your loved one to do his or her best every day.

Write a Letter

For many depressed persons, it is difficult to put into words what they are going through. Sometimes, instead of expressing one's thoughts verbally, it is more effective to write a letter explaining the disease. A sample letter follows:

Dear Family and Friends,

I know I have been acting strangely lately but I am suffering from clinical depression. I am writing in hopes you will understand.

This is a mental disease that may cause me to say or do things I regret later. I want you to understand I love you all and need your understanding while I battle this disease. It may take months—even years—to recover but I am determined to do so.

In this difficult time, you can help by including me in your daily plans, remind me of doctors' appointments, and take medications as prescribed. Also, understand I may suffer from extreme fatigue and may need your help to "get going" during the day.

Most of all, please be there to listen. I don't expect you to have all the answers, but sometimes I need to get things off my chest.

Finally, even though it may be some time before I recover, don't reject me.

Please understand that I did not choose to become depressed. This disease strikes millions of people every year. But, with your help, I will make every effort to recover and your support will help me to once again become my "old self" or even better!

Sincerely,

Depressed Dan

How Do I 'Get Going'?

For those suffering from clinical depression, just getting out of bed in the morning can be a difficult task. What follows are some ideas that may help you "get going".

Get Out of Bed

Don't lay in the same place all day. Make it a small goal, if you must, to get up and move. Lying in bed is a real temptation because it is comfortable and prevents you from facing the day. But staying in bed only worsens depression. Try to get up and go to bed at the same time every day.

Easy Access to Lights

When you awaken, have lights where you can easily turn them on. This light will encourage you to get out of bed and get moving. Open shades and greet the day as a new challenge.

Make Your Bed

Make your bed so you are less likely to crawl back in. Once you make the effort to make your bed, you may be discouraging yourself from having to make it again if you crawl back in.

Wash Up

Some people find it refreshing to wash up with cold water. Try it. And while you are at the sink, brush your teeth. That is also refreshing. Again, make these small daily goals if you must.

Use Self-Talk

Talk to yourself in a positive manner to get ready for the day. Tell yourself the day will be a good one and motivate yourself by getting out of the bedroom or off the sofa. Every day can be a new adventure!

Set An Alarm

Don't hit that snooze button! Some people say they wish the snooze button was never invented. Try to get up as soon as you wake up.

Have A Good Breakfast

Start your day with fuel for your body. Making a special breakfast can also be a small goal.

Most of all, it gets you into the kitchen and makes you less likely to hit the bed or sofa.

Listen To Lively Music

For some, the music they listen to reflects how they feel. Try some lively music selected to get you moving. Music can also keep you awake and keeps you away from the television (note that sometimes it is a good mini-goal to watch television but one can watch too much). If you have a clock radio, program it so that you wake up to music that helps motivate you.

Set A Small Goal

We have already covered small goals so try setting one for yourself. If you accomplish that small goal easily and early in the day, select another small goal.

Get To Bed Early

Try to maintain a "normal" sleep schedule. If you go to bed late and get up late, you may miss out on the best part of the day. You may also miss out on opportunities to visit friends and family.
Resist the temptation to nap during the day and, instead, "save up" your "sleepy" time until evening hours.

Watch Medication

Don't take medication that makes you sleepy only to sleep during the day. Take your medication as prescribed but if you are prescribed a sedative-type pill, see if you can take it towards evening. Consult your physician or psychiatrist if necessary.

Exercise

Make exercise a regular part of your day. It may be particularly useful to exercise in the morning so as to get the blood moving. Again, make this a small goal if you must.

Remember that exercises do not necessarily require special equipment, videotapes, or strenuous moves. Some people even create their own exercises.

Note that it may not be a good idea to exercise just before bedtime. It may be more difficult to fall asleep if your heart is racing. Give yourself time to "wind down" from a workout.

A word of caution, before engaging in strenuous exercise consult your physician, especially if you have a heart condition or other serious health concerns.

Call A Friend

Tell a friend that you need to talk (even briefly) to help you get motivated during the day. Call that friend as part of your daily routine or, if

Depression is often a lonely illness. Do not focus on the darkness but rather the light that shines through.

necessary, have that friend call you at the same time everyday.

Talking about the day ahead will help you set and accomplish goals.

Set Deadlines During The Day

Tell yourself that you are going to accomplish a certain task by a specific time. Set reasonable deadlines and try to attain them. But don't get discouraged if you fall short of your goals. Remember that tomorrow is another day and you can set new deadlines.

Make A Plan

Having a daily plan is a good way to get motivated. It doesn't hurt to write the plan down each day and post it where you will see it. When reading these suggestions keep your mind open to new adventures. Here are some suggestions for planning your day:

- Make and keep appointments.
- Go to a drop-in center.
- Clean at least part of your house or apartment.
- Go to work. Working or volunteering can greatly help one with self-image problems.
- Volunteer.
- Exercise.

- Watch television Again, don't spend the whole day doing this but some television is okay, especially if it motivates you. If you think you may be watching too much television set a time limit for yourself.
- Go shopping. You don't have to spend money to have a good time at a shopping mall.
- Visit family or friends.
- Go touring. Get in your car and have an adventure, even if that adventure is as simple as going to a shopping mall to watch people. Any busy place can help distract from clinical depression. Consider a train station or busy airport.
- Prepare a special meal.
- Read. Your depression may make it difficult to do much reading because of lack of concentration so select an easy book or magazine. And instead of trying to read the whole publication at one sitting, break it up—even if it means reading only one paragraph at a time.
- Go to a Bible study group or read the Bible on your own. Look at Psalm 71:14-24 for inspiration.
- Do some chores. Take the garbage out, wash windows, clean the refrigerator, mow the lawn or shovel snow. Tasks do not have to be difficult to keep you going during the day. Make your chore list short so as not to be overwhelmed by it.

- Do crafts or other hobbies. If you don't have a hobby, go to a hobby shop and explore. You may surprise yourself with a hidden talent!
- Take a special trip. Plan on visiting a place you haven't seen. Get out a county or state map and plan a trip to new territory.
- Play a sport. Shoot some baskets with a basketball, play softball, or go bowling. Join a sports league, if necessary, it will give you an opportunity to meet new people.
- Help others. It can be very gratifying to help others in need. Examine your strengths carefully and explore how you may be able to use them to assist others. You may wish to volunteer at a school, deliver meals to the homebound, or serve meals at a soup kitchen.
- Go to the library. Examine new books or browse through magazines. The point is that it is important to get out and do something different.
- Go to a movie. Matinees usually cost less than evening shows and don't be afraid to enjoy yourself. Besides, no one will see you crying in the dark.

Recovery

Because each person is unique, so is depression and recovery. For some, recovery comes about quickly. For others, it may take many months.

Either way, recovery is possible and one should set his or her goals for recovery carefully.

Symptoms may ease gradually or abruptly. Some people feel better almost immediately after their first therapy session or after they have taken early doses of medication. This improvement may last until full recovery or it may wane; much of this depends upon the cause of the depression, its depth, and the attitude of the sufferer. But many feel better because they were finally diagnosed with a problem and have committed themselves to improvement.

Don't be frustrated if symptoms abate gradually. Remember, for most people, you didn't get into depression suddenly and recovery make take time.

Instead, focus on the good days when symptoms are less noticeable. And remember that more and more good days are ahead if you maintain a positive attitude, take medication as prescribed, and follow the advice of therapists.

Eventually, you will find that you are having more good days than bad. And, ultimately, you will find your "old" self again ready to meet new challenges with the determination you used to recover.

Generally, depression symptoms do not disappear in the order they appear. Usually, it is the most recent symptoms that wane first. Look for gradual improvement in symptoms and follow the advice in this book to overcome the most difficult times depression imposes.

What Do Doctors, Hospitals, Medications and Psychotherapy Have to Offer?

Doctors, hospitals and medications are all part of the mental health picture. Although related, each plays a separate role in helping the depressed person recover.

Doctors

When you have a heart illness, you go to a cardiologist. When you have an eye illness, you go to an opthamologist. When you have a mental illness, you should go to a psychiatrist.

While many family physicians diagnose and prescribe medications for clinical depression, the best place for expert advice is a psychiatrist. A psychiatrist is a medical doctor who specializes in brain function. But general physicians can play an important role in recovery.

It is important to rule out a physical cause for what appear as depression symptoms. A variety of illnesses and conditions could cause these symptoms and laboratory tests are frequently required to rule out other problems.

Once accurately diagnosed, a referral should be made to a psychiatrist. Be certain to tell the psychiatrist exactly what is going on. If the psychiatrist doesn't listen, consider a new one.

What follows is the story of how one mentally ill person was finally able to communicate with his psychiatrist:

Bob had suffered from depression for several years. Despite his best efforts, he felt unable to talk to his psychiatrist. He always felt as though he were mumbling when the doctor asked what was wrong.

"I was brought up to respect doctors so I was always nervous when I went to see the psychiatrist," Bob says. "I was afraid to tell them exactly what was happening to me."

Finally, Bob wrote a letter to his psychiatrist and memorized the letter. He practiced reciting the letter to friends until he could say it perfectly.

On his next visit, Bob recited the letter and handed the psychiatrist a copy. The psychiatrist was surprised but finally understood the depth of depression Bob was facing.

A new combination of medications was prescribed and Bob is now on the road to recovery.

Although highly educated, psychiatrists aren't mind readers. You must be entirely open and candid with them if they are to help. If you are nervous or reluctant to share information with a psychiatrist, do as Bob did—write it down. Then practice it if you must.

Be certain you keep both family physicians and psychiatrists aware of <u>all</u> vitamins and medications you are taking, even aspirin. This is because some medications interact with others and can have serious side effects.

This is also true for herbal medicines and supplements—including the highly publicized St. John's Wort. Let your doctors know what you are taking so they can make the best decisions for your treatment.

Hospitals

Mental hospitals provide an important function in the treatment of mental illnesses. It is here that new medications can be tried and patients stabilized. Some hospitals also provide group and one-on-one counseling.

If you are suicidal, don't be afraid to say so even if it means hospitalization. There is no guarantee how long one spends in the hospital but they are unlikely to release you until you are feeling better. Generally, hospitalization for depression is somewhat less lengthy than for other, serious mental illnesses.

Hospital staff also looks for a plan for after your discharge so that you are safe and don't need to return right away.

If you have a crisis plan (discussed earlier in this book), this is the time to implement it. Take the plan with you or have someone deliver it to your treating psychiatrist. Discuss it with hospital staff.

Unlike mental hospitals of the past, as are often portrayed in movies such as One Flew Over the Cuckoo's Nest and Sling Blade, modern facilities often provide a positive treatment experience. Staff are trained to listen to problems and keep you comfortable.

One treatment worth noting is electro-convulsive shock therapy (ECT). This involves the sending of electrical currents through the brain, which can then reorganize itself.

ECT was once a popular depression treatment but fell out of favor due to drawbacks, such as short-term memory loss. Today, however, ECT has been refined so that only portions of the brain are affected. ECT is regaining favor as it is painless (although it may be uncomfortable for a short period) and can be very effective for severe, chronic depression.

In most states, ECT cannot be used without a patient's written permission.

Many patients who enter mental hospitals for the first time are frightened. But consider the fact that repeat, voluntary stays are common. This shows mental hospitals can provide a positive treatment experience.

Whether to go to a mental hospital is a decision best left to the patient. Many, many depressed persons do not need this extensive treatment but, if you do, it is best to try it with an optimistic attitude.

It is important to note that people with depression may become suicidal and/or homicidal to the point where safety is an issue. In these cases court orders for involuntary hospital stays may be required.

To stay out of the hospital, consider the following list of things one can do (note, this list is similar to others that have appeared in this book but some suggestions are worth repeating):

- Keep busy. Keep your mind occupied and off the problems your depression has brought.
- Take medication as prescribed.
- Take control and responsibility for yourself. Decide that you are <u>not</u> going to get worse and make a plan around that decision.
- Avoid negative thoughts such as guilt or shame.
- Attend counseling sessions and consider a support group.
- Socialize. Get out and be with people. Nothing can help you keep your mind busy more than getting out of the house with friends and family.
- Act early. Notify your doctor, social worker, or nurse that you are having problems.
- Take classes (hobby, academic, or vocational) to keep your mind active, create new challenges, and meet people.
- Avoid negative situations and people. Surround yourself with positive people.

- Be optimistic. This is often extremely difficult for the depressed but it can be done.
- Get up and get going. Challenge yourself to attain goals—even very small goals.
- Plan an outing. Plan a good time for the future.
- Write a letter or in a journal. In a letter, tell a friend how you are feeling or keep track of your feelings in a journal. In a journal, you can always look back to remember that bouts of serious depression don't last forever.
- Get an adequate amount of sleep. Don't "hide" in your bed all day but be certain you are getting enough sleep as discussed earlier in this book. If at first you don't succeed in falling asleep, keep trying.
- Eat right. Eat a varied diet with plenty of fresh fruits and vegetables.
- Avoid caffeine.
- Avoid alcohol and illegal drugs.
- Listen to soothing music.
- Exercise. Try a brisk walk to energize your day.
- Review and understand discharge information from your previous hospital stay, if any.
- Maintain physical health. This means more than exercise. Take medications as prescribed and avoid unhealthy foods and behaviors.

- Volunteer. Put your problems aside and take on a new challenge. Consider volunteering at a hospital, zoo, botanical garden, library, or school.
- Go to church and get involved. Don't underestimate the value of spirituality.
- Make crafts—paint, carve, mold, whittle, draw, etc.
- Be kind to yourself. Remember to reward yourself with a trip to the tanning salon, beauty parlor, or baseball game. And don't feel guilty about it!
- Read.
- Apply for a job. You can learn a lot and have fun just applying for a job. Focus on the job-application experience if you are not ready to work.
- Pray for strength, good mental health, the well-being of others, or anything else on your mind.
- Visit someone who understands depression. You may be surprised to learn how many people suffer from depression. Visit them and share your feelings and experiences. If you don't have anyone who understands depression, make the effort to educate them.

Medications

Fortunately, there are many new medications on the market to effectively treat clinical depression. These include Paxil^{TM},

Wellbutrin™, Effexor™, Zoloft™, and others. And there are signs that a whole new crop of anti-depressants may soon arise due to recent depression research.

Generally there are few side effects with anti-depressants. They do not slow you down or make thinking any less effective. Most are designed to increase favorable chemicals in the brain. Many of the new medications are called selective serotonin reuptake inhibitors (SSRIs) and boost the amount of serotonin available to brain cells.

As mentioned earlier, new research indicates that actual parts of some brain cells may be damaged, which causes depression. Researchers are now studying this phenomenon and new medications designed to help heal these damaged brain cells may result.

Medications don't work unless you take them. A common complaint among doctors is that patients either stop taking their medications or only sporadically take them. This is especially true of the clinically depressed because it takes a certain amount of commitment and energy to remember to take medications.

Also, some patients take medications for a few weeks and, when they don't notice improvements, stop taking them. Be aware that it may take as long as two months for therapeutic levels of medications to build up in the blood. There are no "quick fixes" to depression and this is true for medications.

It is important to take medications as prescribed because doctors need this consistency to evaluate the effectiveness of medications. If one anti-depressant isn't working, then they may prescribe another. Sometimes it takes months, but eventually doctors usually hit on the right combination to help you fight depression.

Another class of drugs that can help fight depression is monoamine oxidase inhibitors (MAOIs). MAOIs are sometimes prescribed for those who struggle with deep and prolonged depression.

MAOIs are not favored by many psychiatrists and physicians because they have many side effects such as sleep disturbance, low blood pressure, and weight gain. Also, many other medications—especially SSRIs—cannot be taken in conjunction with MAOIs. Finally, some foods should not be eaten while taking MAOIs.

For extreme cases of depression, however, MAOIs may be prescribed—especially if the client does not wish to undergo ECT treatment.

Be aware that some anti-depressants have side effects. While these side effects are often temporary, they may include: dry mouth, constipation, bladder problems, sexual problems, blurred vision, dizziness, and drowsiness during the daytime.

If you experience troublesome side effects, do not abruptly stop taking the medication. Consult your physician or psychiatrist for advice. Remember that, in many cases, side effects are temporary.

Recently, there has been much interest in the use of herbal medicines, particularly St. John's

Wort (*Hypericum perforatum*). This plant grows in the wild as a low bush with yellow flowers in the summer.

St. John's Wort is widely used in Europe; in Germany, it is the most widely used medicine for the treatment of depression.

Currently, the National Institutes of Health is conducting a long-range study of the effectiveness of this herb. But in 2000, the U.S. Food and Drug Administration issued a Public Health Advisory regarding St. John's Wort.

The advisory said the herb appears to affect an important metabolic pathway used by other drugs to treat a variety of illnesses. As a result, it is vital to consult with your physician before taking any form of St. John's Wort.

About 15 years ago, Prozac came on the scene. The medication has many positive attributes and has been prescribed widely to combat clinical depression. It is simply one more weapon in the arsenal to fight depression.

Again, be certain all of your doctors are aware of all the medications you are taking, including aspirin and herbal substances. Also, the range of medications available for nursing mothers is somewhat limited.

The medication therapy for children and adolescents deserves special note. Although many "adult" medications are prescribed for these young people, the U.S. Food and Drug Administration has not adequately studied the effects of many medications on children and adolescents.

Encourage the physician and/or physciatrist to use caution when prescribing medications for young people.

Be Aware Of Other Illnesses

Clinical depression takes its toll on the body. It is not uncommon for other illnesses—particularly diabetes—to emerge. Several studies suggest that those with diabetes may be twice as likely to suffer depression.

Treatment for depression in the context of diabetes should be managed by a mental health professional—for example, a psychiatrist, psychologist, or clinical social worker—who is in close communication with the physician providing the diabetes care.

This is especially important when anti-depressant medication is needed, so that potentially harmful drug interactions can be avoided. In some cases, a mental health professional that specializes in treating individuals with depression and co-occurring physical illnesses may be available.

People with diabetes who develop depression, as well as people in treatment for depression who subsequently develop diabetes, should make sure to tell any physician they visit about the full range of medications they are taking.

Remember that both depression and diabetes can be treated simultaneously and successfully.

Psychotherapy

This type of therapy is often referred to as the "talking cure." It involves the use of a psychologist, social worker, or counselor and generally referred to as a therapist. It could be a pastor or someone trained in treating mental illnesses.

Psychotherapy can help one learn how to cope with the strange feelings and actions depression can bring. A therapist can also help one manage symptoms.

Moreover, therapists can help the depression sufferer understand the thoughts and feelings that brought on the depression. For example, they can help a person understand how to better deal with anger or grief.

Therapists can be found in the yellow pages under "mental health" or by word of mouth. A pastor, physician, psychiatrist, or health plan provider can also help locate a qualified therapist.

It is the job of the therapist to listen and offer support. While the best therapists are those who have actually suffered the disease, qualified therapists are trained to offer advice.

Some mental health agencies use peer counselors—people who have had experience with a similar mental illness. These paraprofessionals can play an important role in "validating" feelings—assuring you that what you are feeling is "normal" for a depressed person. Also, knowing someone who has conquered the disease instills hope.

Because therapists are trained listeners, it is important to be completely honest and open with them. If you are hearing voices or having similar hallucinations, tell your therapist. Also tell them if you are feeling suicidal.

You should quickly develop a trusting relationship with your therapist. If you feel he or she is not listening to you, try another therapist.

There is a stigma associated with psychotherapy. But this stigma should take a backseat to seeking help with depression. Remember depression can be fatal without proper treatment. Educate friends and family so they will understand your desire to see a therapist.

In Conclusion...

If you are reading this book, you most likely have acknowledged that a problem exists and have decided to get better. Pat yourself on the back because those are two important steps to recovery.

The primary message of this book is hope. Although life may seem hopeless right now, hope is out there and, if you keep your mind open, will find you.

Remember: You are not alone! Your feelings may seem strange—even bizarre—but millions of others suffering from clinical depression have felt or are feeling the same things.

Also remember there are many mental health professionals who can help you toward recovery.

When you recover you should keep your mind open to new opportunities. For many, it is like "starting over" and while one may have lost a job, a marriage, or savings, recovery could open new doors never before explored.

Millions of people recover from depression and so can you. Follow the advice in this book and give yourself the opportunity to enjoy life again.

For More Information...

      For information about local resources, look in the Yellow Pages under "Mental Health."

      More information about clinical depression is available by contacting the following nonprofit organizations:

National Depression and Manic-Depressive
Association
730 N. Franklin
Suite 501
Chicago, IL 60601-3526
Telephone (312) 642-0049; (800) 826-3632
http://www.ndmda.org

World Wide Web Mental Health Page
http://www.mentalhealth.com

American Psychiatric Association
1000 Wilson Blvd.
Suite 1925
Arlington, VA 22209-3901
Telephone: (703) 907-7300; (888) 357-7924
http://www.psych.org

North Carolina Alliance for the Mentally Ill
http://www.ncami.org

Canadian Psychiatric Association
http://cpa.medical.org

National Institute of Mental Health
Information Resources and Inquiries Branch
6001 Executive Blvd.
Room 8184, MSC 9663
Bethesda, MD 20892-9663
Telephone: (301) 443-4513
FAX: (301) 443-4279
Depression brochures: (800) 421-4211
TTY: (301) 443-8431
http://www.nimh.nih.gov
E-mail: nimhinfo@nih.gov

National Alliance for the Mentally Ill
2107 Wilson Blvd. Suite 300
Arlington, VA 22201-3042
Telephone: (703) 524-7600; (800) 950-NAMI
http://www.nami.org

National Foundation for Depressive Illness, Inc.
P.O. Box 2257
New York, NY 10016
Telephone: (212) 268-4260; (800) 239-1265
http://www.depression.org

National Mental Health Association
1021 Prince St.
Alexandria, VA 22314-2971
Telephone: (703) 684-7722; (800) 969-6642
FAX: (703) 684-5968
http://www.nmha.org

American Psychological Association
750 First St. NE
Washington, D.C. 20002-4242
Telephone: (202) 336-5500; (800) 374-2721
http://www.apa.org

Center for Mental Health Services
P.O. Box 42490
Washington, D.C. 20015
Telephone: (800) 789-2647
http://www.mentalhealth.org

Depression and Bipolar Support Alliance
730 N. Franklin St.
Suite 501
Chicago, IL 60610-7204
Telephone: (800) 826-3632
http://www.dballiance.org

Depression and Related Affected Disorders
Association
Meyer 3-181
600 North Wolfe St.
Baltimore, MD 21287-7381
Telephone: (410) 955-4647

National Alliance for Research or Schizophrenia
and Depression
60 Cutter Mill Road
Suite 404
Great Neck, NY 11021
Telephone: (800) 829-8289
http://www.narsad.org

National Mental Health Association
2001 North Beauregard St.
12th Floor
Alexandria, VA 22311
Telephone: (800) 969-6642
http://www.nmha.org

American Academy of Child and Adolescent
Psychiatry
3615 Wisconsin Ave. NW
Washington, D.C. 20016-3007
Telephone: (202) 966-7300
http://www.aacap.org

American Society for Adolescent Psychiatry
P.O. Box 570218
Dallas, TX 75357-0218
Telephone: (972) 686-6166
http://www.adolpsych.org

Depression After Delivery, Inc.
91 East Somerset St.
Raritan, NJ 08869
Telephone: (800) 944-4773
http://www.depressionafterdelivery.com

Postpartum Resource Center of New York, Inc.
109 Udall Road
West Islip, NY 11795
Telephone: (631) 422-2255
http://www.postpartum.net

Depression/Awareness, Recognition and Treatment
National Institute of Mental Health
5600 Fishers Lane
Rockville, MD 20857
Telephone: (800) 421-4211

Dean Foundation for Health, Research and
Education
2711 Allen Blvd.
Middleton, WI 53562
Telephone: (608) 836-7000

National Mental Illness Screening Project
One Washington St.
Suite 304
Wellesley, MA 02181-1706
Telephone: (781) 239-0071; (800) 573-4433

Americian Association of Suicidology
Telephone: (800) SUICIDE
http://www.suicidology.org

About the Author

Steve Harrington earned a bachelor of science degree in wildlife biology from Michigan State University. He also earned a *juris doctor* from the Thomas M. Cooley Law School. He is currently studying toward his master's degree in social work at Grand Valley State University.

Steve has lived most of his life in Grand Rapids, Michigan, his current residence, but has had many adventures. These adventures include floating a log raft down the Mississippi River, photographing polar bears in the Arctic, participating in black bear research in northern Minnesota, canoeing in the Canadian wilderness, and rock climbing in the Colorado Rockies.

He works for a mental health agency as a consumer advocate and counsels clients suffering from clinical depression and facilitates depression support groups.

Steve has written for many publications, including The Detroit News, USA Today, Outdoor Life, and has written ten books on wildlife, legal issues, shipwrecks, and scuba diving.

"Nothing has brought me greater pleasure than helping people battle depression," he says. "It is a terrible disease but watching clients recover is very rewarding."